DEAD SALMON DIALECTICS

Copyright © 2014 by Derrick Stacey Denholm.

01 02 03 04 05 06 19 18 17 16 15 14

All rights reserved. No part of this publication may be reproduced, stored in a retrieval system or transmitted, in any form or by any means, without prior permission of the publisher or, in the case of photocopying or other reprographic copying, a licence from Access Copyright, the Canadian Copyright Licensing Agency, www.accesscopyright.ca, 1-800-893-5777, info@accesscopyright.ca.

Caitlin Press Inc.
8100 Alderwood Road,
Halfmoon Bay, BC V0N 1Y1
caitlin-press.com

Text design by Kathleen Fraser.
Cover design by Vici Johnstone.
Cover art by Derrick Stacey Denholm.
Printed in Canada.

Caitlin Press Inc. acknowledges financial support from the Government of Canada through the Canada Book Fund and the Canada Council for the Arts, and from the Province of British Columbia through the British Columbia Arts Council and the Book Publisher's Tax Credit.

Library and Archives Canada Cataloguing in Publication
Denholm, Derrick S., 1969–, author
Dead salmon dialectics / Derrick Stacey Denholm.

Poems.
ISBN 978-1-927575-58-1 (pbk.)

I. Title.

PS8607.E625D43 2014   C811'.6   C2014-904125-X

Dead Salmon Dialectics

Derrick Stacey Denholm

CAITLIN PRESS

The stories people do tell about land are multilayered, and do not lay out explicit ecological knowledge isolated from other aspects of life. As is common in storytelling traditions, the information—the meaning—in a narrative is up to the listener to decipher.

—Leslie Main Johnson

Poems flow toward consciousness.
A poem is an amplifier of information
that is not a continuous series of images
but a grainy wave
transmitted in packages of possibilities.
The implicate order of a poem
connects everything with everything.

—Ken Belford

The things themselves are not what science can reach ..., but only the relations between things. Outside of these relations there is no knowable reality.

—Henri Poincaré

1.

    no obstacle
        "all living is a meeting"
            mediated by invertebrates
                fungi   bacteria
            each   a physical process
              a means
              inevitability

        if art   really is a dream
        a nutrient-recycling pathway
          she   should not limit herself
to human views
        domesticated by the excretions
            of traditional composition

    when studying rain salmon in streams
    toward the awakening of minds
        the blind gumboot poet/ecologist
            must make herself
            clairvoyant

        when one thousand rain salmon tell her:
            "time is a landscape
            years are a revolving world"
        that "it's an event geography"
        that life is the avocation of the world
    she records that this may be the most crucial
    yet not the most obvious perspective

as around, above and away from her
not all branches sway in unison

(while the nearby stream edge
courses that sidewalks
return shin splints

2.

    too close to the sticks
    to go for the throat
    of omnivorous nature
    in the north coast tangle
        of stream edge
        and terrestrial biota
        of industry executives
        and *gum-see-wa* froth

    whether via plant or biofilm production
    many ecosystem processes
    have savage teeth
    ready to influence
        the "bottom-up" effects
        of rundown waterfront hotels
        under the strong, sure discipline of seasons

    (while one nurse log conifered a few jokes
            about ecosystem food webs
            about the honest commitment to knowledge
        that were not funny   at various trophic levels
        that seemed to have no impact whatsoever
            upon rain salmon nutrient dispersal
            or grasping the tropes of north coast pragmatics

we should now know
that we must not think
any girl who talks as coherently as that
            on the bus
                on the scale of a whole watershed
        will be stared at
        as though she had green hair

3.

individual lives are only
part poetry

      the consumption pathway
      adumbrates all: the awkward indirect reportage
      by which rain salmon biomass
      incorporates partway
      up and down phloem   into trophic webs
      "to detach our desire
      from all good things   and to wait"
      through the feeding stream
      the watching forest   the breathing estuary

individual lies are only
partial disruptors:

    settlers
    immigrants
    colonialists
    transients
    conformists
shifting places on a map—the throwaway x:
    fly-camps of wifi tin
    plastic, wireless
    rare earth elementals
    each gravel scrape
    a finger-peeled scab

freedom and entitlement   cuts
more looping   thoughtless trails
    shrugged by the buckle of frost-heaves
    the grey two-lane of asphalt
    bisects the past from the future
        for natal streams
            for water   rushing   away
                as we polish our teeth
    emptytime biders
    aliens amongst the echo
    yaw   and sigh   of young cedar
Hagwilget old   *'Ksan* flow a tree
        as Wittgenstein almost describes:
    the bumps intellect acquires
    running her head up against
    the limits of language

where individuals live
        it is all that is communicable:
        within immobility and silence
    and   it is all over prince rupert
        that she had a nervous breakdown

both hinge upon both:
>   externalised context
>   internalised incest
where going out is going in
with no easy characterization
>   where rain salmon biomass
>   along its directional flow
>   of the assimilating overburden
>   is not an unfelt experience
>   but is a larger-than-human perception
>   a living sensation
>   of memory, love and awe

top-down or bottom-up
"this" is a cynosure   proposing
>   more complex assessments:
>   that rain salmon trophic systems
>   are regulated by myriad pathways
>   that without having to read a specific signature
>   she knows a repercussive cursive when she feels its cuss
>   that sometimes she must use a poem as if it were a broom
>   or something heavier

4.

    anadromous
        rain salmon   natural in conditions
        load the upstream enormous
            (as nutrient streamlines
            serve dynamic conduit systems'
            ascription of carbon
                nitrogen and phosphorus

  where accessible habitat
       is to suitable distribution
       as input-derived marine materials
       are to freshwater and terrestrial systems
       mainstream poetry
       as often becomes automatic
       and protects itself
       against any and all thought
       as easy as a newbie
       falling off a (b)log

(as Snyder assays:
    "as climax forest is to biome
    and fungus is to the recycling of energy
    so 'enlightened mind' is to daily ego mind
    and art to the recycling
    of neglected inner potential"

    thus   rangy   gilled
           from portland inlet
           up the *Kiteen*
           the anadro*must* re-enter in
           access smaller and smaller
           tributaries and disperse
                     (deeper than particle physics
                     and what the occident has fixed
        as true
              up tiny headwaters
           stream a living thread of flesh
           as far as far as far in and to the interior
                through mouths, fur, wings, limbs
                    and thought

just as the difficult
        non-picturesque poem
        runs its mathematic of water and stone
        where nothing comes easily
        within which—as "they" say—no beauty lingers
        where ignorance repeats its own
            emptinest
            palimpsest

5.

    as rainforest fluvials
    fan to receive
    fewer salmon
                    poetry
    remembers/resists/registers
    the small brown tracks
    of voles and various other
    detritivores—those who will not find
    what for, why and how come
    of the living infinite
            upon a finite page

    of the thousands of things
        we always forget
    millions of larger-than-human things
        accomplish the three Rs
        from   *to*   and   *of*
        even the smallest of streams

    may this practical and useful past
        pass in ongoing currents
        beg positive order
        from rubric statistics
        translate ecological phenomena
        beyond the inverse/obverse
        antipode of reference order tools:

      spring forces
      drag forces
      generalized fisheye views
      separation caching
      garbage collection
      centralization
      homogenization
      the efficiency strategies
      of devolution

  where so often
  cultural understanding
      becomes a compost library
      of distortion techniques:

"I was mad. I was angry. I was happy"

"frightened by the carcass of this huge monster"

"setting aside an acre of land for habitat conservation for every acre of wilderness permanently impacted"

"to dull and eventually stifle our intellectual and aesthetic capabilities, our creative perception, and our use of language"

"with only a paper-like cut across her left hand, and perfect hair"

6.

> *Kitlope*
> *Nii Luutiksm*
> *Gilaxkyoo*
> *Ningunsa*
> *La̲x'wiiyip*
> *Xaaydziks*
> *Lax'nasiis*

decolonizing waters
without the dysgenic names
that legislate resource development
        and "provide a predictable revenue stream
        for local government and jobs
        for both Aboriginal
        and non-Aboriginal people"

(just   as elder George Jim spoke:
        "these fathers of mine
        who were enchanted
        by the Coho spirit.
        I don't want it to have to lie unattended."

pellucid and circinate
impeding access
from high-elevation freshwater
terrestrial ecosystems
down data mountains
to the oceanic industrial
rentals and repairs
with the distribution of equipment
parts and fuel supplies
concrete, gravel and building materials
clearing, logging and salvage
      an extensible force-based
      physics simulation
      enabling increased scalability:
      a skitter viz using hypviewer

7.

    (jurisdictional
            conceptual boundaries
        remain, conceal and inhibit
    (within the animated
        radial
        graph
        layout

    (while rain salmon are meant to move
        riverine
                (against
        the mainstream
        starfield display

    (to   diffuse spawning grounds
        to percolate the landscape
    (despite scalability
        in the thousands
        of onscreen items

(autotelic
biomass widely distributes
    its graphic transformation of
    panning and zooming inputs
        (per square metre
   ecosystem nutrients
      (per squall retreating
   increasing up low-order watersheds
      (pulsing in/to
        the headwater reaches
        of hi-res colour maps unfolded
    and then impossible to refold
  (the truncation
of marine-derived
   nutrient distribution
     (as caused by log dams
       and habitat destruction:

  (proprietary layouts
  (bifocal distortions
  (graphical fisheyes

in downtown terrace
she steps on the naked spinal comb
of a smoked, recently eaten sockeye
which lies in the dust beside a metal post
which she knows is where
it should not be

8.

        this phloem (
       written
   (for the mossed conifer
        multi-podal
north coast
        estuary tangle

    wafts
                              nothing
        but
           the characteristic

        white

         of page

     quickly forgotten

9.

        of the rain
        forest rain
        estuarial dusk
        rain dark to dawn
        a pellucid meniscus break
        a *Noctiluca scintillans*
        microscopic flash
        of rain flint
        against stream
        water steel

        hemlock redcedar cypress
        branches sieving/winnowing water
          drop   green/silver keystrokes
              wet verbal runs
                    rain indefinites
                weighty drippling articles
    nudging   subsurface   plankton

            electric
                              light
strike
                flash

        splay

            & fade

        upstream
      rain salmon bump
   rainbow static off lateral lines
    tails highlight the run
    flow in cursive nonfriction
    with passive keels
    a spatulate fin blade
    reduction of yaw
   rolling the pelvic/pectoral
   prompt to hooked kypes
   jog of phosphorescent echo
   shimmer and fade
   body outlines with pale flit
   along under and down
   rainfall's gravity surge
    the flipping returns
     of endlessly wret pages
     to the estuarial dawn
      of rain
       forest
        rain

10.

…
if something
so transparent
as the appropriate use
of a conjunction
meets an opaque wall
(never mind a watershed
where each drenched moss
intention in twisted ulota or dusky fork
swims with a rain salmon reality
from the mind of the pacific
to register here, up and down
within *Tsuga* xylem and phloem
read in multiple directions
written for intervention and necessity
of *Stlindagwai* night-fisher bears
elaborating darkness ÷ water
+ stones × cold (with no concept
of time except this fish in mouth
and much more than the momentary desire
to rip the heads
from relentless marine muscles
who re)write themselves up
natal streams of *Gaxitaga'dsgo*
the web-intimate hieroglyphics
of ecosystem health

just a few of the thousands
of guide-tropes (by which
spawning salmon ÷ bears
+ secondary consumers
= rainforest trees ÷ water
re)cycles to correct choice
(of appropriate use
when demonstrating relationships
between correlative clauses
and the human tendency
to wander, grope and blunder
lured by the din of machines
to each fresh, gaping maw
... how do relentless marine muscles
perform achieve attempt miracles
reveal more than the mere datum
of an arrival essay
and maintain the diversity
of the ancient genetic phrase
of blood-cartilage memory
with nocturnal torpor response
and resistance
to the night prompt and pounce
of starvation-threatened bears
...

somehow
some *Klickaskoon* keta
avoid the barest movement
and live a few more hours
to, somehow, mate, spawn and die
hatch, live and return
…

to revise
to rewrite
to reconsider
the appropriate use
of conjunction
…

11.

        tracing
   nose-braille networks
  multi-generational trails
  indelible footpad marks   idiomatic elements
  of ecological grammar   (wound amongst the random
  nurse log windthrow ambiguities of collapsed text
 reclaimed by elderberry devil's club goatsbeard lady fern salal
  false azalea salmonberry   transmitting messages
 denoting *Khyex* river referents below hemlock spruce alder
 cottonwood redcedar phrases   of non-erroneous form
 edging the adaptive interface   of rain salmon streams)
   having slept away most   of the consonant daylight
 to nightfall's blind rain sweep fisher bears plod in slow assonance
 grope into the elusive glimmer   blunder the flow to dislodge
  one of evolution's sluggish   mate-paired *thunnus-esox*-form
  rain salmon night clusters who resist the constant estuarial pull
  with paired hydrofoil fins   (another evolutionary adaptive
 reciprocal fit for negative lift   in stream-mark station holding)
 black at the stream-edge black rainforest bears fumble-scatter-select
   out of those closest given   those flashing a bright halo trace
dart to reveal processual expression and content in the black unmoving
and with one night scoop bioluminescent splash/bite of twice as much success
   as those rainforest bears   fishing daytime's jar and confuse
   in the sunflecks' harsh cast   amongst the raking branch
                            jangle reflection
                            of water surface
                               distraction

12.

just as nutrients refer *although* to various marine-derived commons
rain salmon image affects *of* as the first mistake of gumboot science
whereby an ecosystem-derived *from* conforms *with* to consumer needs
in confusion with a clear demarcation of *which* as the limit of poetry's surprise
leaving typical salmon postcardisms to reside in subsequent surveys of *be*
which spawns *where* to degrade beauty's otherwise veneer trump value
even as ministry reports rupture *whatever* onto paper as poetry-deep lakes
streams and forests reconfirm *has* as the ineffable failure of a concrete *by*
thus incorporating *because* into rain salmon tissue as the legal form of *unless*
which recognizes *in between* as two species-specific *of*-type pathways
and accelerates *either-or* up the food chain unless *against* directs consumption
and dilutes *should* with *among* for both terrestrial and freshwater limits
upon all sedentary harvests of *must have* while an abundance of sea-run *as if*
coincides with an even more predictable aversion to *whatev* as it decomposes
along a well-stratified leaching below *with* to signify the final excretion of *until*
which renders all remaining carcasses into *such that* scattered across *inasmuch as*
in contrast to *while*, even as nowadays we mainly say "please excuse me" *wherein*
back in the old days *except* would validate *have* with a cuff to the poet's head

13.

    rainorcoastrain
    salmon
    straining the wet seam
    reveal ground-truth   a drenched
    Gilttoyees fern   let go
    listening   to a hung-up hemlock   at last
    plough its whale bark   into moss   rain

    Qol-q!a'lg.oda-i
    "mouldy forehead"
    a remarkably dry X̲*aaydaa* teen
    once called
    her various diagrams
    and doodles   entering the food web
    the countless denotata
          (she packs around   not just in her head
          a scrawl written up and down
          samples of data strewn across spiked green leaves
          pink cartilage "dross" over rooting epiphytes
          red gill rakers combcurved into the little hands
          of liverworts cold-sorting the specific nature
          of rain salmon–derived nutrients
    all biases of the syntactic "backlash"
    Nature has in store

as rain salmon continue   to die
downstream   clogging the estuary
she continues   to work
not writing   something definitive
    but a preparation
    a flesh-something-out
        of in-stream biomass
        and out-stream poetry
      where science interpenetrates
        how she sees herself
        amidst so many carcasses
        disintegrating

within a misstep
wet boot imprint
she sees a foot-long tapeworm
    flail for its life
    within a mound
    of fresh grizzly shit:
        half   cooked devil's club berries
        half   cooked salmon cartilage
            & this one pale limp bone

wet
her eyes widen
        underneath
        fifty hundred
        blackgreen
        tiny hemlock
        wing hands
        waving
        for more rain

14.

noting processes:
                    larger consumers
                    smaller microbials
     the results of intuition results   in conclusion
          a need   for conk lesions
          protrusions of polypores
          up and down an amabilis fir
          a fat green-grey bank of nutrients
          a darkness warmth of decay a dead and dying yew
          a clenched-wood and whorl-twigged medicine
          a life renewed   in/within thirty
          or three hundred
          bewildering phrasal years

and a dramatic variation in the fluctuation of biotic consumers

"the Real Work"
where nothing/everything happens
          literally on paper through each literati stage
up water
down through so many dying and dead salmon
decomposing their philosophy of gravity:

the essential inevitability
of stream-tumbled gravel
a theory of phloem   where everything *is*/changing
a practice in poetry   where wording/image
re-present/change/rot
through the black veins of skeletal leaves
compiling what has been
              written/red/dead

while
at a desk
within four walls
behind a small glass
and against the grain of life
the core sampling
of increment bore truths
often turns into
"I don't like this"
as soon as
"this is not the way
I could imagine it"
moves to the side of art
where absolute
endings begin

15.

now is then
: the importance of dispensing
with pseudo-scientific paradigms
; listening to those who speak
"in a voice too quiet for panic to hear"
; through the fast remembrance of heavily leached soils

11,064,750 ha.

and almost real   she works toward eco-logic
upon a lambert azimuthal equal-area projection
and prints out alluvials, glacials, mors, moders and mulls in 2D

    : active within litter, fermentation and humus
    values under a thick layer of diverse mosses
    ; within wetter meanings deeper than meaner dupings
    at each hundred-year-old flaking scab along the highway

        : alive, a 500-year-old bronze tree
        hollow, a 1,000-year-old silver snag
        and down, the 2,500-year-old deadfall gold
        rotting above a spawning channel
        where rain salmon entanglements
        disregard stream "escapements"
        educate desires and inspire practices

    : independent sample tests   (two-tailed
     f-ratio tests   (two-tailed
    fall   to the null hypothesis
          of equal variances
          above and below
          falls and watersheds

                                (within the living tail
                                (of intestinal residents

meaning is mapped in
where watersheds link
to the terrestrial *where*
where a stream-leaning pistol-butt fir
taut her that edge effects
can initiate cornerstone cascades
that misguides always fly in formation
that wild animals can see
all the saturday night sledneck debutantes
in pink, lime & baby blue camo
all the way back in smithers

16.

      while early scandinavian physicists
      affirmed that the aurora borealis
      was an offshore phosphorescent glow
      cast off by large schools of herring
much earlier   in the spawning cycle
      north coast rainforest bears
      salmon wolves   salmon otters
      and various other species large enough
          to capture ripe rain salmon
      feed voraciously upon the facts
         of the living re)discursive
         eco-logic of the lipid-rich

(never too hungry for immediate keta solutions
     to the problems of seasonal starvation
     streamside place aesthetics
     and cohesive ecosystem maintenance

concerned not only with the movement
and intensity of evolutive processes
     but also for the need
     to survive until spring
wild Indigenous bodies
     (those that live and die
     the decompositional marine-nutrient trophic
     within a community schema
     of gravel, rain and hemlock trees

re)declare, perpetually refine
the official unfinish
    of competition and cooperation
    for the finest tropes of the salmon forest
    later and later into the spawning cycle

the cultural work of the various salmon fishers
    scavengers and detritivores
        —the many unsung protagonists
        of biotic affirmation—
    renews the age-old-all of the rainforest
as they feed upon the live eggs
    the live and rotting carcasses
    and the marine-nutrient outfall
    of a constant flesh slurry
    that slowly diffuses downstream
    : these historic, geographic
    and geopsychic properties
        of *Ishkseenickh*
        Ksi Sgawban
        Exchamsiks
        Quilgauw
        Ksadagamks
re)model themselves into theoretical references
    within the increasing surplus
    of disintegrating remains
    within a salmon-forest paradigm

one that suggests alternate intimations
    escape routes
        out of contemporary history
    and expresses innovative re-conceptualizations
within new-old prescriptive models of the Wild
    that serve water, sky and land

    while human business-as-usual
    continues to promote and reward
    ever hungrier techno-rationalist
    cost-cutting wealth chasers
    those whose manipulative visits
    by internet and aeroplane
    to north coast communities
    are verbiage dismissive
    buy-off and sell-out
    neoliberalist programmatic
    abyss-front destructions
    of all "Real Work"
    disseminated through a series
    of mainstream prosperity manoeuvres
    the increasingly lush poetics
    of an ecology of bad ideas
    the herring phosphorescence
    of an irreparable
    industrial catechism
    of corporate cliché

17.

    (she looks up from her duksbak
        and thinks again
    watching a dripping cypress schoolmarm
    demonstrate many important points:
        one, that increment bore frass
        indicates more than the holes in a poem

up to a certain syntactic
   in the aftermath of spawning pragmatics
   she wonders: is it true
       that rain salmon   (like ecological science
       scattered in their tropes
       across the forest floor
can suspend dying   and dead designata
       to intellectual particulars   of unreality
   just like poetry   with its similar field
       of rotting carcasses
       (after having gifted
       and depleted their energies
can they all work to renew
       the average energetic/emotional tissue
       replenish intuition and conscience
       with sea-run   wildput and output
       from the diffident   to the ambivalent
       and crucial throughput of the Wild

bringing forward an ethic beyond precise disciplinary data
    of quantifiable conclusions
those very same ideals
        that stoic   salient science
        demands of her report?

        one hardsoft
        purplebrown cone
        checking wonder
        falling down
            once more
        at the big picture
            asks
        a divergent question

18.

    tropes
        of rain salmon
        recycling
intent
on the energetic that detaches
    from between the lines
    of aesthetic preoccupations
    within freshwater transformations

the rain salmon   is neither text
                      nor artefact
    not even one of millions
    of ancient anadromous words
    but a living flutter/shudder
        whorling the renewal of itself
            within a gravel bed
                of natal ephemera

```
like the phloem
she     is concerned with the long-term
            nitrogen contents
            of truth-standing poetries
            more than the so-called music
                    that registers
                        as


                            the intertext


                passes through


    editorial process
```

19.

    personally ambivalent
    yet impersonally delighted
    with ironies   eco-gnomics
        organic abstractions
        excreted by living fish
she takes   and gives   downstream notes
    (wondering
    if this is any more
    than rain salmon lip service
    the discontinuous staghead discursive
    draped in wet moss
while the first inorganic nutrient
    ammonium (NH_4^+)
scrawls its erose way into streams
develops new "ugly" qualities
of repetition and frustration
shortly after spawning mortality

a week or two later
levels of ammonium   sentience
    new existential configurations
    soluble reactive phosphorus
    experiments in the suspension of meaning
having leached from carcasses and gametes
    and re)released during spawning
    re)increase in stream water

upstream
pre-confederation edits
    re)redcedar log dams
revise her fluid position
to, of and from
    the downed tree-stance
    of intellectual relativism
rewriting the abdication of everything
    r)ending the auld skool idea
        that anything river ends
        with its completion
    thus re)imagining and imitating
        ancient Other methods
        of the estuarial re)cycle
        re)return of life to the sea

which is just

20.

    beginning
        next season's
        fluvial paradox

adult rain salmon re)write
    ascend runoff
    and sea-salt glacial melt
    transcribe outputs inputs throughputs
    under a log criss-cross   ring pellia-deep
        chiasmus
    post-spawning   re)palimpsest
    a red-bryum-on-salmon-nutrient-salmon-on-red-bryum
    tidepool   ebb flow   in situ   rot

dead rain salmon in streams
continue to stream with their imaginative advantage:
    ammonium
    and signal recognition particles
        (the ribonucleoprotein complex
        essential for co-translational insertion
        of proteins into membranes

like the phloem   an email   or a poem
rain salmon   decay and disintegrate
    input rite into ecosystems
    aspire without conclusion
    build up Belfordian lan(d)guage
    gift nutrient an unlimited effort
    create successive interpretations
    imply a share of meanings
    accumulate untold cumulative
    community effects
    and become susceptible
    to various kinds of rulings
    for any number of user tasks
        : data-scions within balloon tree layouts
        decking platforms for interactive visualizations
        alpha male–stage bug-testing
        built-to-order custom skidder applications
        binomial grafts for degree-of-interest tree handfallers
        rundowns for speed-dependent automatic zooming
        snag brushing, waste repositioning & decay indexing
        spar tree virtualizations for integrated search functionality
        which benefits   in the construction phase
            : "4,100 person-years of on-site employment
            31,300 person-years of off-site employment
            2.5 billion dollars in total labour income
            165 million dollars in tax revenue to government"

      when   only anadromous skeletal tissues
              remain as auto-referential
              existential   assemblages
phosphorus and calcium
      still engage the irreversible duration
      drift   and reside   as echoes
              as a logic of intensities
              scattered as nutrients within bones
              that drift beyond the edge effect
              of redundant   virtual
              consumer streams

21.

scattered
to plentiful
shallow accumulations
of organic soils
in shaded crevices
between stream-edge rocks
phosphorus logbooks
through average runs
of spawning rain salmon
a wet counter soraismus
lichen breeze discursive
script to the "normal"
ordering of "things"
meeting or exceeding
the shade-tolerant work
of subcanopy epiphytes'
indifferent effort to defamiliarize
the hunky-dory idiot strings
of "authority" ideology
crown to branch to root
to fungus to stone
to stream-out
to a counter-repetition

a *Stó:lō* girl
named Stacey
wearing a t-shirt
that reads "go home"
the intensive disruption
of established
perception habits
replacing both
fatalistic passivity
and get-rich-quick schemes
with circumpolar ferns
submontane liverworts
cosmopolitan shrubs
transcontinental forbs
submaritime mosses
spray-tolerant
evergreen conifers
interconnected
with fresh to moist
to very moist
semiterrestrial
wet cool
mesothermal
marginalia

22.

        this is not a poem
        commonly found
        on the ground
        after windstorms
        to sit and read
        directly but a running
        streamcourse to decipher
        in the round
        deep consonant flux
        of entropics
        water-shedding
        and water-receiving
        wringing out the senses
        in specific sites by season
        within annuals shifting
        opposite beside before
        Other larger-than-human
        entities whose occurrences
        increase with increases
        in precipitation
        distance from power lines
        indifference to logging in
        from the other side
        of the logged-off
        edge interface
        a minor literature
        engaging Land
        as gift

23.

    lost
    never mind
    her watch purposefully
    scattered to plentiful
    in closed-canopy
    coniferous forest sensitivity
    to the pang of dividing the Real
    into a number of discrete exchanges
    for a handful of acid organic
    substrate redrot under scissor-leaf
    liverwort testes of a male
    rain salmon stripped   discarded
    by a discerning   not-quite-black
    Gitnadoiks bear   preparing pragmatics
    of stream-gravel-time
                in preparation for winter
            having given up on shopping
    her stories about walking single
    phrasals cycling in the millions   the locus
    from the *Golim'aks* to the scots-owned estuary
    to powell street industrial ports on the lower east side
    streams filled in or shunted blind through concrete ducts
    under bus lanes   factory fluvial outfalls
    fenced-off waters
                seeping through cracks
            to wash rust brown pilings

sea to sky and back to *Nilkitkwa*
water-shedding onto fresh
nutrient-rich soil just as this poem
is not nice   not the psychologically safe
landscape image   a quick and easy
wordcandy frass for those who don't like to get
              their feet or anything else wet
                     those whose watches
                        should be retired
                              better yet
                                   lost

24.

    dead
    spawned-out
    Slamgeesh rain salmon
    float   drift   and sink
    the ready breadth
    of phosphorus to epilithon
        (the microscopic
        organic matter that
        attaches to rock surfaces
        science reports
        and government
        regulations
providing these and other non-charismatic tropes
        (biodegrading and
        ordinarily crossed out
        rather than let stand
        on the stream-edge page
            (underneath 50m to 60m
            and often taller
            sitka   cypress
            redcedar charismatics

a glossolalia of critical invocation
for ever-deepening intensities
of colonization of the Other
within new existential configurations
    where the rhythm
    of stream to town
    is put left to write
    as biotic sense
    reconstructs itself
    with understanding
    being the feel
    for the rhythm to jump
    bravely through
    and get one's feet
    right what into how
wet upon to and within
the most crucial tropes
of the rain salmon
recycling trophic

(just as mental ecology
reconsiders/rewrites
/engages minute oscillations
from the downtown poverty interface
of a cultural complex
like prince rupert or masset
and the rich hypermaritime
mesothermal of every nearby
Tsimpsean stream flowing in
      (leaving
      mental footprints
      in gravel and moss
      and humboldt bifurcations
      in phloem

writing right off the page

25.

    where
    are energies found
    for acts insipid to sweet
    depending on site conditions
    personal taste
    access to wireless
    connections scattered
    over organic substrates
    in coniferous rainforests
    resonant with raven song:

      croaks
              clicks

gronks pipops

            doyyungs   *hreev-linns*

        blårrttuus   *wob-lumms*

tlöömfs   *klapooks*

                        oouckle-frumps

            pliting-flinoos

              skrraaaaa

where
for more flexible renderings
of usability evaluations
in mixed communities
with nothing apparent
in common to counterbalance
perspectives between
water-receiving sites
under closed-canopy forests
for developing yet another
start-up natural-form mimic
web design company
striving to bully the relentless
ephemera of internet buyers
with newer and newer
blankety blank-box commodities'
relentless jackass manufacturing
rootless obnox waste commodities
a daily confrontation
with a kick
of her boot   in the dank
                           puddle
      the diaphanous
      subjective
      dialectic

dead salmon
decomposing
in the *Kitsault*
in the *Exchamsiks*
the *Gingeitl*
the *Kinskuch*
the *Zymagotitz*
the *Iknouk*

rivers where
across virtual landscapes
stamping variable graph paper
emboss upon non-negotiable zones
breeding season timeflow charts
finite spawning windows
for anadromous returns
crucial venue riparians
of third-quarter season
wildlife habitat feeding patterns
that cannot accommodate
shareholder demands
for third-quarter
              returns?

how can she answer
accept   go back
begin   read a gain

26.

    look in   Dr Out
    insectivorous
    riparian
    passerines
    thrive
    in greater densities
    along the phenomena
    of the natal stream reveal
    a rain salmon-borne
    marine-derived nitrogen
    the ancient
    phylogenetic experiment
    cycle clock of the long here
    perpetual wonderings of *where*
    is your dictionary? instinct
    motivations of propitious
    evolutionary corollaries of now
    in pragmatic conscious decisions
    occurring amongst
    interacting wild communities
    bird allsorts unlocking
    your hat with natural response
    survival system pivot
    dodge and spiral floooo
    hiding

      in basal rosette
        swamp lantern
          oblong-elliptical corydalis
          coarse-toothed sitka
          valerian lance- to spoon-shaped
          shootingstar loose umbel
          mountain sweet cicely
        shaggy hairy nootka
      lupin wing-stalked
    rusty saxifrage

look out   Dr In
to the natal stream pulse
of invertebrates produced
through the abundance
of decaying salmon
demonstrations
of themselves
the gift proof data
that there must
be a tearing out
not just of pages
but that something desperate
must not *take* place

displacing the auto-reification scourge
of homogenous upholstery moulderings
an electric horsehead
licking the molten core
dry-humping the one-dimensional
linoleum of place
both stupefying and infantilizing
fervent corporate hybridizations
the consumer consensus trait of another
where is my reaching-the-plateau reward?
cut into carefully indexed phloem
pages torn out
to roll choice
doobs   smoke out
cells   instead of growing
free streamside improvisation
where "salmon squirting through"
suspend absolutes of meaning
revegetate both industrial-scrape helicopter access
and the denuded halogen-flood management
of the once-TSA-thirsty overstorey

even if she could find
a triple-prong blackcurrant bush
with surge protection
she knows that a google search bar
can do little *in* the *Damdochax*
won't reify a twig; but *to* it?
virtually, Dr In answers to Dr Down
whose algorithms
are watertight

while water itself remains open (
all sea-run typographic prominences
spawn-shaded understoreys
are a musicolous flow
of elevation persistence
within open-canopy last stands

27.

(for Harriet Nahanee

    value and identity
           gift
    through imaginative stories
    the carrying capacity
    of rainforest bears   increasing
    under cool   temperate
        dripping wings
              of mesothermal
              coniferous rainforests
    where rain salmon energies
    spawn population densities
    up to 80 times greater
        not merely according
        to what someone
        is devised to cost
        or how much
        something
        is willing to pay
    overwriting   long-term
    ecological processing fees
    costs hidden   in phloem
    deeper   in gravel change
    perpetuating natal-stream culminations
    raining back downstream
    for which some rain salmon

```
rainforest bear      salmon forest        ecosystem
estuary     ocean        inchoate human
         will receive a bill
                  despite
                  one
                  riparian
                  witness tree
                           who
                  rainsong sings
                           that she
                  is a refusenik
                           floated
                  eagle down
                           gift
                  into
                           her hair
```

28.

    the marvellous capacity
    to grasp between
    reproductive success
    and mutually distant realities
    attributes to more
    than post-spawning
    transversal theories
    of salmon nutrient availability
    for poverty-stricken consumer-entities
    such as:

eagles	ecologists
otters	loggers
bears	feminists
wolves	antiracists
ravens	poets

frugality gleaners
of wild-gift knowledge
with season-to-season
kincentric scrawl spark and bloom
all nitrogen-rich
denudata juxtapositions
of vegetation structure
    within the proximity
    of runoff channels
    along steep-gradient
    stream-edge rainforests

where
rotting carcasses
play foraging activity
systems of reference
amongst terrestrial vegetation
against the insidious repetition
enforcement of incorporeal production
power centre decisions from vancouver
toronto new york tokyo london beijing
sell and buy Others by online invoice
that each order of singularity
must be:
    evaded
    turned
    or crushed
by the pressure of specialist economic apparati
seamlessly disseminating both ideology and force
within a coagulate mass of popularized memory
that demands:
    utilization
    repression
    and death

29.

    she is no fan of poetry
    especially this kind
    which strives to articulate
    salmon-borne
    marine-derived nitrogens
    in interconnection
    with new-old aesthetics
    recycled analytical practices
    a renewed vision
    as microscopic prose
    writ in litter-level mosses
    saprophytes
    understorey shrubs
    where the staked-out
    midstorey plot centre GPS'd
    within forests of trees
    old-growth epiphytic lichens
    liverworts and forbs
    perform the Real Work
    distribute the rotting flesh
    of systemic thought
    as much as 500 metres
    from natal streams
    to library shelves
    in basic rowstacks
    where textual memory
    and reports collect dust
    and degrade quickly

                    yet between
the *Gilttoyees* and the *Quaal*
redrot ledgers crumble
in unseen grand mute proof
slowly sinking
under plume
and glow
moss drenched
within acidic soils leaching

squeegeeing these putrefacts
of fish residue
into ziplock bags
         (off of sword fern fronds
          spiny brands curving giant
          palmate-leaved devil's club
          minute rain-shedding delicate
          maidenhair spleenwort
she   is a face in the trees
committing seasons of years
to the biotic processual
puzzling and pasting together
         ecosophical fragments
             from excerpt quotations of rot

all essential for organizing methodologies
creating vernacular technologies
hope for incremental policy shifts
new-old micropolitical
and microsocial practices
commitment to solidarities
and a new-old gentleness
gifted from what is Indigenous
growing a contiguous
interdiscipline
within shade-tolerant
submontane to subalpine
very wet to moist
perhumid sites

read by a mossy few
the poem
as phloem moving up
living as xylem moving down
within a seasonal series
of energy sinks and ethical shocks
green words mainly unseen
unheard in form and content
with no immediate profit return
undervalued
underpublished
all eventually
redrot underfoot

30.

    although it may seem to drop wakefulness
                    upon her alone
    terrestrial vegetation also responds
    to the ambiguity of the poetic/ecologic text
    to the plankton light of her small step into a salmon stream
    the poem arriving—suddenly making things life-sized
    breaking into small intuitive missives
        of semi-local comprehension
        out of cosmological responsibility
        if not a wholly concurrent meaning
            that no longer imposes
            the resolution of opposites
yet reveals the crucial role of the foraging activities of bears
 where before the rain rang things not unsaid
 its wild editorial   still transmitted messages
                    denoted referents
      all responded to by communities
            of scavenging invertebrates
                  detritivores
                  and microbes

while a filament burns
upon her seat
back in the dam(p) office
before the datum presence of rotting salmon carcasses
integrating so-called redundancies
        of expression——————— — · —— · — · · — · · — ·
        herstory————————————————————— · · ·
        and content—————————— · · — _ · —— · ·
trinomial lines that dissolve
amongst terrestrial vegetation
as if her response was based on fact
over which her overdue poem/report
must take precedence
at the drop of a gill raker
out of the top
        of a spruce tree

31.

she compiles pragmatic irresolution
after indications that riparian tree growth increases
where salmon-derived nutrient inputs sieve and flow
                up through phloem

while amidst the academic scrawl of copular denotata
the bi-engendered sugary vitamin photosynthate
refusals of power continue up and down the vascular bundles
                of ancient living intertext

despite the fact that so many have resisted developing an
ethic of responsibility and remain in the generalized larval state
one in which the average reader cannot say with any confidence
                that they even exist

she scrawls upon this wilfully discursive branch of ecosophics
not just for the satisfaction of out-of-the-way aesthetic wordplay
but for the sake of out-of-the-way sites within cool mesothermal forests
                where bear foraging activities occur

within the wide profusion of dynamic, atypical growth
where streamside vegetation is influenced by marine-derived inputs
expressions of a wet-word dialectic of disintegrating flesh
                resound within forests rain-loud and large

fast where standing people shelter natal streams
she chooses the earthy flavour of sound wood and succeeds
slowly working amidst the unexpected inflorescence of poetry
                      in an attempt to bewilder heartbreaking readers

    biotic/creative event intrusions
    make the poet/ecologist drift
    away from her previous path
    no longer impervious to realizations
    of value shifts along stream-flow forms of conduct
    not just within the perhumid estuarial
    moist shade of grey and green
    but more importantly
    in response to an overburden
    of ecological largesse
    within largely urban institutions

(as an 800-year-old hemlock crashes
rain twig needle shock & clamour
the whale-sized piano smash of litterfall
into her plot—3 metres closer
would have flattened her—she
re-recognizes the relativity of scale
here along the bedrock scrape of the *Kiskosh*
with its pulverizing, multi-limbed, random response

this biotic gift of ethical weight
where marine-derived nitrogen
rises within terrestrial vegetation
enables canopy patterns of optimal shade
to nurture natal streams
where redrot barriers regulate flow
reach diffuse for ravens to perch
to pick and redistribute carcasses
return them in finite scraps
where they come from and recompile
reminding her to witness
and then start to breathe
once more

32.

living ancient
sea change eco-logic
silver rain salmon
freshen water run red
-purple-brown-green-grey
are torn to shreds by wolf
bear and eagle and drift
belly-up to fix the eddy
with nitrogen, bleach white
and sift downstream the radical
complete gifts of prime self
streaming in broad dispersals
within the competitive cooperative
of north coast biotic ecosystems
ever looping to flush and revise
decentring models of recycling tropes
into the ecotone aesthetic
of the perhumid estuarial riparian
phylogenetically refining tree-shrub-fungi-
microbe-crustacean-nematode culture
creating richer LFH accumulations
deepening and diversifying
the forest floor with salmon buttresses
of true fir, hemlock, redcedar and spruce
enriching biomass down in the carbon sink
for raven-scratch twig-fall larvae-fly

the many robust perennial essays that uncoil
their wild cursive by rain breeze in low cloud
nurturing the stout practical green
by increments of rhizomatic encounter
in stark rainforest contrast
to the roiling servile
parallax and churl of fear
the factory-line nature of subjectivity
and intensifying capitalist power
mediations of industrial pressure
that encroaches with its synthetic monoculture
of cheap downloadable commodities
of 3D laser overproduction
landfills swelling past glaciers' decline
widening the extent
of the unsettling ponds
of progress

33.

    wet downtown
    socked-in mist
    city of rainbows
    fading sparks
    of capital flight
    on *the Way* back
    from not-shopping
    she picks a path
    through the fishlike bodies
    of empty glass bottles
    scattered, gills gaping
        shattered

    she "laughs"   (again)
    at irony's long distending
        death
    thinking   (once more)
        of Others

bones disintegrating
cartilage dissolving
into the infinitesimal
percolation nourishment
of a 1,000-year-old redcedar bog forest
where tiny outliers of symbiotic association
with newly forming mycorrhizal fungi
build bi-directional transfers
of nitrogen-based nutrients
under mossy nurse logs
along branching mycelial pathways
one cell wall thick
here where the *Tsimshian*
worked for generations
to push waves of *Gidaganits* raiders
back to their northern fjords

      arriving at her apartment
and standing under a mossy window
along the sledneck rut strip
she finds another wall-scrawled threat
in the dark
      giving no value
      representing nothing
      except a totalitarian order
      that can only be obeyed
      with its own destruction:

"Drink Coca-Cola"

34.

    underfoot
    Hydnum repandum
    Gomphus clavatus
    Russula xerampelina
    Dermocybe sanguinea
        all partners
        in the rhizomorphic
        mycelial matrix
    broke it down for her

: growing another year
to kneel the soaked litter layer
deepening layers of woody debris
bacteria, corollary levels of microbial
fungal structures wending, tending
        all to the upheaval of the status quo
        in this house of water
        decomposing the grafted
        the plotted, the played-out
        the mass media imaginary that underlies
        canadian industrial society
        weeding out, rending, underwriting
        the clear formation of the unconscious

all providing timely food sources
for rodents, herbivorous insects, worms
a variety of cover for small mammals
nesting birds, amphibians, arthropods
the rain-soaked, the ecologist, the poet
the degraded, now so soft underfoot
original knowledge and culture
a synchrony of ecosophical praxis
gravel-covered eggs, arthropod
skeletons, the micropolitics of desire
wind-weather and water-words
a sea-run terrestrial-borne understanding
of anadromous participation
with bioluminescent exchange
night-fisher bears hunting salmon
by the torchlight of plankton

clenching purposeful distance
from transcendental supervision
and mass-market meat production
watching things thinging and unthinging
high up on public walls in the dark
she clenches isolated singularity
turns askew/askance in repressed circles
this third world within the first
peering downwind of its own backfiring
deregulation, lack of security, lack of meaning
all of western history's
negative disturbances
of, for starters (and enders)

interconnected terrestrial vegetation structures
deregulating the boles of uncounted riparian trees
into supplication for whole log exports
the deregulation of the amount of light
needed to shade natal streambeds
and breathe life into in this house of water
   leaning back
   against wet bark
   shivering
   under a hemlock safe
   she knows she could
   never be a fan of anything
   and still be
   what she meant to be
   while these wooden tumblers
   locked in resin
   slowly loosen her mind
   to engaging processes
   of "heterogenesis"
   to enabling
      the singular
      the exceptional
      the rare

   and closing her eyes
   for another moment of shivering

   (and in between is where
   the frayed edges become visible
   within mainstream space

35.

mental ecology
: a larger-than-human transect
plots its epiphytic ethic
across the perhumid eco-logic
of subcanopy soil mats
that store water and
provide pre-objectal
support for sky roots
midstory foliage
and absorb pre-personal
fog and rain

this primary process
where rainforest bears
take up to 80 percent
of the entire spawning logic
into the humo-ferric run
of an included middle
into a glaciofluvial coexistence
disintegrates the meanings of
the beautiful and the ugly

an aerial ecosystem
of fern and huckleberry
supplants the mesoslope idiom
of upper canopy life
: copepods and salamanders thrive
the redcedar-hemlock crown
where black and white absolutes
become rainforest indistincts
working to overgrow roads
with a seemingly indiscriminate
moss repair of the good object
and the bad subject
the most isolated coastal islands
and the broad hecate lowlands
where salmon forest vigour
always smells like the dead fish
of rotting money

36.

    sensation offshoots
    of storied land
    spawn-mar the wave tug
    of a hecate strait pulse

    late summer's deep metallics
    cycle into olive-barred horns
    a freshet catalogue of full-body kypes
    nose/claw drafts of salmon bear cartography
    : locate/snatch in jaw
    black paw forest sketches
    expressive-path frameworks
    of these singular night-fishing rituals
    : perceive/receive/precisely singularize
    the gravel-scarred phantasm
    of instinctual eco-logic
    : spawned-out & half-eaten
    bones raking even the thinnest organics
    back over bedrock

when spawning returns abundance
the logic of nitrogen ideas is not contained
within upstream psychologies
of the downstream surge
organizing into "instead" systems or "minds"
a blue-green push, the constant arcane splash
their boundaries defined by ocean currents
and participant terrestrial consumers

diacritical exclamation marks
and scattered flesh actuates
the root text stria
: wet vegetation understoreys
old-growth logbooks
marine-climate theses
all are a mere passive anecdote
industrially manipulated
by the expurgative pressures
of integrated world capitalism

37.

    although they prefer the brains
    of spawned-out females
    when migratory returns shortage
    the actions of salmon bears
    enunciate more than the particulars
    of subsystem theories of "context"
    perforating the diverse
    stream-keen torque
    the inconsistent persistent
    heterogeneous rhythm-to-plot schema
    of rough-spent migrants
    salmon bears claw up unabridged drafts
    consume whole ragged copies
    yet always expurgating
    the text(e)s of the male
    littering the forest
    with his shredded
    shrivelled prolix

38.

under ideal conditions
the perpetual fog and rain
ritual of the season
rainforest bears eat far less than half of their catch
each bear depositing up to 700 dead salmon
beyond purely abstract information
within the deep perhumid mosaic
of saprophytic orchids
across the stunted wet forest and acid bog
1,600 kilograms of urgent vitality
a rainforest refertilization
scattered along path tangles
of the tri-ecological dare
to make a vertiginous cosmos inhabitable
to bring into being
Other worlds:

    in heavy shade
    reduced to thin
    semi-transparent
    sheathing scales
    white or creamy
    to greenish white
    coral-like rhizomes

in poetry
a *Kts'mat'iin* bear—one rainforest trope
—distributes dead salmon
to the point where the composite text
decides the interconnective play
conflates meaning into relative capacities
to live/recognize discursive chains
of ecological imbroglio
        for up to two martens
        four eagles, twelve ravens
        150 glaucous-winged gulls
        and up to 250 crows
—all singular operators
crystallization elements
within the recycling trophic
signifying fragmentation chains
        (which Schlegel would call "works of art"
            : hundreds of snaggle-toothed jaws
            fixed within metaneckera
            spiky rib combs embedded
            in white-toothed peat
            armoured gill coverlets
            lodged in curly thatch

all fjordland forms of storytelling
within which her glaciofluvial assiduity
aims to convey not only the essential nature
of marine-derived nitrogen in phloem
    (as in the data of her report
but to de-decibel the arena rock argot
asset-stripping afterhours party
that ruts up the agnostic narthex

and these post-industrial
tasks of decomposition
: to relight a sporadic buoy
to reorient the coastal ecotone disjunctive
to underpin the whorled navel view
    (where natal streams
    have become the new drop-off points
    for the bullet-riddled bodies
    of urban gangland hits

the poet/ecologist
gumbooting through Real Work
within Guattarian forms

: a pre-personal letter of intent
where the signature isotope
exhibits itself within the sapwood
of 500-year-old riparian trees
produces new subjectivities
in relation to the Other
the foreign and the strange
wrangles incrementally into policy shifts
accepts wholeheartedly
to "meet head-on
the encounter with the finitude
of desire, pain and death"
  slows
     the machine
phylum
   down

39.

    north of caution
    she slip~
           ~tumbles *Heiltsuk* rain
    dance scrapes moss
                oofs rock
    cracks the screen of her GPS
                kills it
    on the granitic batholith
    realizes that here
               november rain
    is more fish slime than water
    is no love restrained

    that not only are the bones of the *Nisga'a*
    composed entirely of salmon
    but the whole archipelago is a drenched green
    blanket morphology of throbbing red arteries
    woven under drooping conifer murk
    that redcedar flags of *Tlingit* persistence
    drizzle constant seaward migrant smolt
    that hemlocks run *Haisla* returns of keta and tyee
    up and down vascular salmonid cambium
    below a *Gitxsan* lateral line swell between xylem and bark
    that *Sitka* spruce cruise-dart their pollock phylogeny
    around the seasonal kype of the alaskan gyre
    that black bears surge under water under roots
    deep fathom black & white orca life & death
    in the 700-year-old shallows

where silver candelabras scatter-chase
shore pine herring around *Talunkwan* shoals
the vociferous understorey alder screech, dive & swoop
sleek on glaucous *X̱aaydaa* wings over the blowhole
where shining mackerel schools lean 500 years
of marine-derived sapwood over *Kitkiata*
spreading their tiny transparent rootfins
to thrive amongst tinier mycorrhizal connectors
ancient ravens of wood and whale blast a *Quaaalkrrrrr* soar
of *Tsimshian* spring-runs up sockeye-red oxbows
humpbacking the *Quaaal* narrows north to the *Gilttoyees*
a last/first/eternal octopus-root gravel spawn
wet dream flutter and death of cypress decay
up and down the *Kxngeal*

north of caution
november rain   squalls
throw ferns   sand & microbes
grey whales, marten & eel-grass
murrelets, crustaceans & wolves
in scaly purple-hard time capsules
from crown-heavy fur
down through her hair
into the creek
where technology sits
leaking poison

Notes

Some of the poems here have been published in slightly different versions in the *Capilano Review, Contemporary Verse 2, Dreamland, Drunken Boat, filling Station* and the *Goose*.

Tom E. Reimchen's website contains a great deal of useful resources for understanding the relationship between the salmon and rainforests of coastal British Columbia. The writing of these poems was heavily influenced by research into the following studies:

Hocking, M. D., and T. E. Reimchen. "Salmon-Derived Nitrogen in Terrestrial Invertebrates from Coniferous Forests of the Pacific Northwest." *BioMed Central* 2, no. 4 (2002): 1–14.
Reimchen, T.E. "Salmon Nutrients, Nitrogen Isotopes, and Coastal Forests." *Ecoforestry*, Fall 2001, 13–16.
Reimchen, T. E., D. Mathewson, M.D. Hocking, J. Moran and D. Harris. "Isotopic Evidence for Enrichment of Salmon-Derived Nutrients in Vegetation, Soil, and Insects in Riparian Zones in Coastal British Columbia." *American Fisheries Society Symposium* XX:000–000 (2002), 1–12.

The epigraphs at the start of the work:

Leslie Main Johnson, *Trail of Story, Traveller's Path: Reflections on Ethnoecology and Landscape* (Athabasca University Press, 2010).
Ken Belford, *Lan(d)guage* (Caitlin Press, 2008).
Henri Poincaré, *Science and Hypothesis* (The Walter Scott Publishing Co. Ltd., 1905).

Other sources used throughout the work, chronologically:

1 "all living is a meeting," Martin Buber, *I and Thou*, trans. Ronald Gregor Smith (Charles Scribner's Sons, 1958).
"time is a landscape ...," Michael D. Blackstock, *Salmon Run: A Florilegium of Aboriginal Ecological Poetry* (Wyget Books, 2005).

3   "to detach our desire ...," Simone Weil, *Gravity and Grace*, trans. Arthur Wills (University of Nebraska Press, 1952).
    "the bumps intellect acquires ...," Ludwig Wittgenstein, *Philosophical Investigations* (Basil Blackwell Ltd., 1953).
4   "as climax forest is to biome ...," Gary Snyder, *The Real Work: Interviews & Talks, 1964–1979* (New Directions, 1980).
5   "I was mad. I was angry. I was happy," as told by Teresa Chenery, from Brad Cran and Gillian Jerome, *Hope in Shadows: Stories and Photographs of Vancouver's Downtown Eastside* (Arsenal Pulp Press, 2008).
    "frightened by the carcass of this huge monster," a Gitxsan traditional oral narrative, Chief Kenneth B. Harris and Francis M. Robinson, *Visitors Who Never Left: The Origin of the People of Damelahamid* (University of British Columbia Press, 1974).
    "setting aside an acre of land ...," Enbridge Northern Gateway Pipelines, *We're Building More than Pipelines* (brochure, Blanchette Press, 2010).
    "to dull and eventually stifle ...," Alberto Manguel, *The City of Words* (University of Queensland Press, 2007).
    "with only a paper-like cut across her hand ...," as told by Teresa Chenery, *Hope in Shadows*.
6   "and provide a predictable revenue stream ...," Enbridge, *We're Building More than Pipelines*.
    "these fathers of mine ...," Nora and Richard Dauenhauer, *Haa Tuwunáagu Yís, for Healing Our Spirit: Tlingit Oratory* (Sealaska Heritage Institute, 1990).
13 "*Qol-q!a'lg.oda-i*, Moldy-Forehead," an oral narrative by Tom Stevens, chief of Those-Born-at-House-Point, in *Haida Texts and Myths: Skidegate Dialect*, John R. Swanton (Washington Government Printing Office, 1905).
15 "in a voice too quiet for panic to hear," Northrop Frye, *The Educated Imagination* (Indiana University Press, 1963).
20 "4,100 person-years of on-site employment ...," Enbridge, *We're Building More than Pipelines*.
26 "salmon squirting through," Ken Belford, *Pathways into the Mountains* (Caitlin Press, 2000).
38 "meet head-on the finitude ...," Félix Guattari, "The Three Ecologies," *new formations* no. 8 (1989).